# Dividend investing for beginners

# Make passive income with dividend yielding stocks

# Table of Contents

# Introduction

Modern world presents us with a lot of opportunities to invest in financial markets without leaving your home. With a simple push of your keyboard you can buy and sell securities. It is great! However, modern world has experienced a lot of "financial storms", stock market crashes, economic recessions and even collapses of economies. These things scare people away from investing. A lot of investors saw their fortunes dwindle away over a night when markets crashed in 2008.

Fortunately, there are quite safe ways to invest in markets. Investing in dividend stocks has been one of the safest ways of investment for over one hundred years. There are companies that have been paying dividends through the First World War, the Great Depression, the Second World War, all financial crises of the twentieth century and they are still doing that. You will learn about them in the book.

You will also find out about companies that have been increasing dividends for 25 years and more. The last chapter will give you a list and description of companies that have been paying dividends for 50 years and more.

You will also find out all important facts that are important to know before you start investing in dividend stocks. If you are not risk tolerant and search for ways to invest safely I have good news for you. Investing in dividend stocks is for you. Keep on reading…

# Chapter 1

## Benefits of investing in dividend stocks

For hundreds of years long term investors invested in dividend stocks. In the beginning of the 20th century most of the money made in the stock market in the US came in the form of dividends that companies paid to their shareholders. This is one of the opportunities that an average investor can enjoy now too. This age is dominated by speculation in various securities. People tend to believe that they can make a killing in the stock market by selecting a right stock that would rise thousand percent and they will win a jackpot. Unfortunately, most speculators end up losing it all. They ignore long term profits and tend to choose short term strategies to invest in stocks. Very few investors now think about a company in terms whether it pays dividends or not. Most are searching for growth stocks that start their existence in the market from 5$ or something and in a matter of a few years skyrocket to 100$ or even more. They search for future CISCO, Wal-Mart, Apple or Google that are going to fly like rockets to the moon and will make them wealthy beyond their wildest dreams. Very few find these stocks. Some pick up some penny stocks and lose a substantial amount of their money investing in them.

However, the facts speak for themselves. Some say that for the past 100 years or so, more than forty percent of the famous S&P500 returns came from dividends. The statistics should make one think whether it is not better to leave short term strategies and concentrate on the long term ones. One of the best of those strategies is, of course, investing in dividend stocks. When you start delving into the subject you will see how many advantages this kind of investing has over other most popular trading strategies. Let us look through some of the benefits of buying and holding dividend paying stocks.

You may look at the chart from dividend.com to see how much of the profits in stocks come from dividends.

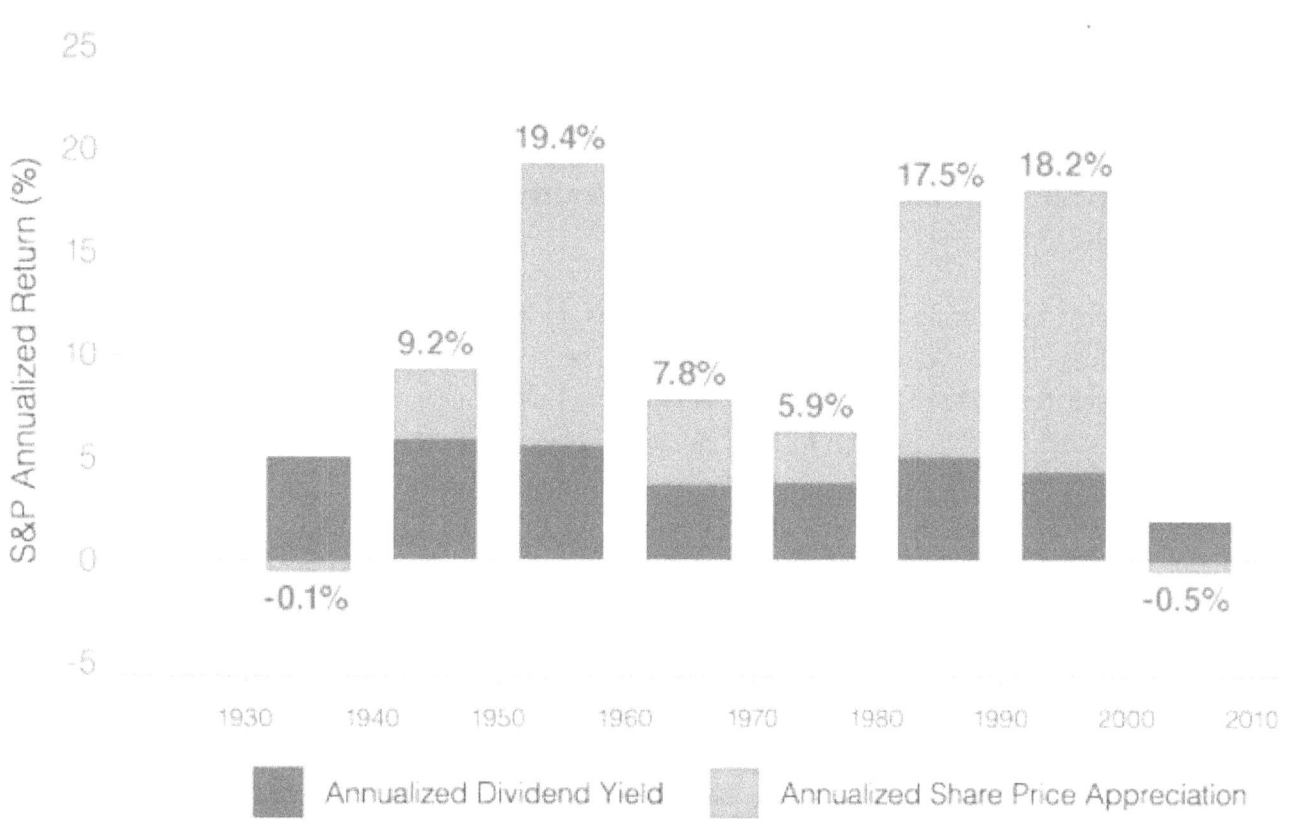

## You earn from dividends and from rising share prices

So, this is a possibility to make money in two ways. Firstly, you get dividends. Most are paid quarterly. Secondly, you can also make substantial amount of money from a rise in your shares. As you know, stocks rise and fall and as you are in these special dividend stocks for the long haul you are surely going to benefit in these two ways: from steady dividends and from rising prices of your shares.

## Steady income year after year

Those who only expect to make money as shares rise will often have to sit out through bear markets when all stocks are falling and they do not get the privilege of getting steady income from the market in those times. Conversely, those who own dividend stocks can enjoy never ending stream of cash in good times and bad. Even if the price of your shares is falling, your dividends are still paid and your steady stream of income never stops.

## The power of compounding of reinvesting your dividends

Some investors talk about the power of compounding when they reinvest the dividends that they get. In a nutshell, compounding is getting earning from previous earnings. So, if you get dividends and you use them to buy more shares of a company that pays them, next time you will get more dividends (and consequently more cash). If you invest those, you will again get more share and more dividends. These earning will keep growing tremendously if you continue doing this year after year till by the time you retire you will probably have created yourself a nest egg.

## This type of investment protects your wealth from losing its value during inflation

We do know that during inflation money starts losing its value. As prices grow your money gets less and less power to buy things due to rising prices. For centuries, investors have tried to protect their hard earned cash from depreciation by investing in gold and also by investing in dividend stocks. Inflation often follows overheated economy when everything is booming and various new businesses spring up. That's when companies make bigger profits and consequently pay bigger dividends. Your price of shares rises and so do the dividends.

## Dividend stocks outperform those that do not pay dividends

Growth stocks may do very well during booms. However, as fast as they rise, they plummet when financial bubbles burst. Those who have held to those stocks often lose all of their profits and even more. Dividend stocks may not take you for such an extraordinary ride upwards, but they will also not take you down hard when economy heads south. So, those who follow long term investing strategies and do not jump in and out of the market trying to get a quick buck earn cash in good times and bad. Value stocks that they hold earn them money even during very bad times, because dividends do not stop coming in bad times. On the other hand, those who have been following short term strategies have no streams of income from the market in bad times and they need to wait for another boom in order to make money from rising prices in stocks.

## These stocks provide you with financial safety and stability

As people grow older they want less risk and more stability and security. That is precisely what investing in dividend stocks is all about. You protect yourself from falling markets by still keeping steady stream of income. Prices of these stocks are often cheaper, but as dividends rise together with prices of shares you earn more and more. In the same fashion as gold, dividend stocks have proven to be one of the safest ways to invest in the stock market.

## It relieves you from pressure of where to enter and exit the market

Short term investors are very concerned as to where they have to enter and exit the market. They intend to capitalize on fast stock price moves and it is very important to be right on time when the move starts. Long term dividend investors do not have to worry about that. They simply select best paying dividend stocks and accumulate their wealth slowly, but surely. They do not have psychological pressure regarding daily market fluctuations as they know they are there for the long haul.

## Conclusion

Dividend stocks are an excellent way to get secure, stable and long lasting income. They will also help you to preserve your wealth in times of inflation, relieve you from thinking about timing of your investing and also help you to earn by means of compounding when you reinvest dividends that you get.

# Chapter 2

## Understanding dividend dates

Dividend dates is part of the logistics of stock dividends and you have to understand these in order to be the owner of dividend stocks before certain time comes. There are four important dates that you need to understand clearly so that you do not make stupid mistakes that will cost you money, simply because you did not know, let's say what ex-dividend date is. Board of directors of a company that pays dividends has to announce all the dates. If you are interested in some company you have to make sure you know when these dates for that specific dividend of the company are. So, let's go over them together.

### Declaration date

Declaration date is the day when the Board of directors announces the dividend. The announcement includes a number of things that all investors follow: how big the dividend is, the date of record and the date of payment of the dividend. After the company announces that it is going to pay the dividend, it is legally obliged to do so.

### Date of record

After the announcement the company also sets a date of record on which or before which you have to be on company's books as a shareholder in order for you to get a dividend. Having done that, the company also makes a list of shareholders that will get company's future proxy statements, financial reports and other important information of interest to its' shareholders.

### Ex-dividend date

After the record date is set, ex-dividend date is set based on the rules of the stock exchange and it is usually done by the specific stock exchange or National Association of Securities Dealers. Any investor who buys shares on or after ex-dividend date is not entitled to receive a dividend. However, the person who sells to him will still receive a dividend. Those who buy shares before ex-dividend date will receive the dividend.

Let's say Procter&Gamble announced a dividend with an ex-dividend date on the 23rd of April, 2015. If you buy shares of the company on the 23rd of April (or after the ex-dividend date) you will not receive the dividend. However, the person who sold you those shares will be paid the dividend. If you buy the shares a few days before the ex-dividend date you will surely get the dividend.

### Payment date

A payment date is the day on which an announced dividend has to be paid. Only those who owned the shares of the company before ex-dividend date will be paid the dividend.

Below is the example of these four important dividend dates. Procter&Gamble company is used as an example.

**Chart of important dividend dates**

| Type | Declaration Date | Ex-dividend Date | Record Date | Payment Date |
|---|---|---|---|---|
| **Date** | 17th of April, 2015 | 23rd of April, 2015 | 27th of April, 2015 | 15th of May, 2015 |
| **Comment** | The date when company announces its dividend | The date you have to be the owner of the shares if you want to be paid the dividend. If you buy the shares on Ex-dividend date or after it you will not be entitled to receive a dividend. | This is the date by which you have to be on the books of a company as a shareholder in order to get the dividend. | The date the dividend is actually paid to the shareholders. |

There are a lot of places on internet where you can check all the companies that pay dividends and find out about dividend dates. You may go to nasdaq.com if the stock is listed on this stock exchange.

If you are interested in Ex-dividend dates you can alternatively go to dividend.com where they have an excellent ex-dividend date search tool, you type the date, order results by Ex-dividend date, stock symbol (alphabetically), stock types and you get a list of companies with their ex-dividend dates. Then hurry up if the ex-dividend date is approaching. Here is a glimpse of how the tool looks like.

**Ex-dividend tool from dividend.com**

## Ex-Dividend Search Options

**Ex-Dividend Date Range:** 2015-06-15    to    2015-06-15

**Order Results By:** Ex-Dividend Date

**Then Order By:** Stock Symbol

**Stock Types:** Common Shares ☑ Preferred Shares ☑ ADRs ☑ ETFs ☑ ETNs ☑ Funds ☑ Notes

[ Search Ex-Dividend Dates ]

## Ex-Dividend Date Search Results

Export Data to Spreadsheet

| Stock Symbol | Company Name | DARS™ Rating | Ex-Div Date | Pay Date | Dividend Payout | Qualified Dividend? | Stock Price | Dividend Yield |
|---|---|---|---|---|---|---|---|---|
| AGM | Federal Agricultural Mortgage Corp | Login/Signup for Ratings | 6/15 | 6/30 | 0.16 | Yes | 31.47 | 2.03% |
| AGM-A | Federal Agricultural Mortgage Corp. Cl A Vtg | Login/Signup for Ratings | 6/15 | 6/30 | 0.16 | Yes | 25.25 | 5.82% |
| BR | Broadridge Financial Solutions | Login/Signup for Ratings | 6/15 | 7/1 | 0.27 | Yes | 52.97 | 2.04% |
| CHMG | Chemung Financial Corp. | Login/Signup for Ratings | 6/15 | 7/1 | 0.26 | Yes | 26.29 | 3.96% |
| CINF | Cincinnati Financial | Login/Signup for Ratings | 6/15 | 7/15 | 0.46 | Yes | 51.65 | 3.56% |
| DG | Dollar General | Login/Signup for Ratings | 6/15 | 7/1 | 0.22 | Yes | 0.00 | Unknown |
| DMB | Dreyfus Municipal Bond Infrstrctr Fd Inc | Login/Signup for Ratings | 6/15 | 7/1 | 0.0625 | Unknown | 11.64 | 6.44% |

If you go to nasdaq.com you can actually find all the above mentioned important dates for any company that pays dividend, plus the size of dividend.

**Dividend dates and dividend size on nasdaq.com**

| Company (Symbol) | Ex-Dividend Date | Dividend | Indicated Annual Dividend | Record Date | Announcement Date | Payment Date |
|---|---|---|---|---|---|---|
| Albemarle Corporation (ALB) | 06/12/2015 | 0.29 | 1.16 | 06/16/2015 | 05/06/2015 | 07/01/2015 |
| Allegion plc (ALLE) | 06/12/2015 | 0.1 | 0.4 | 06/16/2015 | 04/09/2015 | 06/30/2015 |
| AMTEK, Inc. (AME) | 06/12/2015 | 0.09 | 0.36 | 06/16/2015 | 05/07/2015 | 06/30/2015 |
| Belden Inc (BDC) | 06/12/2015 | 0.05 | 0.2 | 06/16/2015 | 05/28/2015 | 07/02/2015 |
| CHS Inc (CHSCP) | 06/12/2015 | 0.5 | 2 | 06/16/2015 | 06/03/2015 | 06/30/2015 |
| Donaldson Company, Inc. (DCI) | 06/12/2015 | 0.17 | 0.68 | 06/16/2015 | 06/01/2015 | 07/02/2015 |
| Ecolab Inc. (ECL) | 06/12/2015 | 0.33 | 1.32 | 06/16/2015 | 05/08/2015 | 07/15/2015 |
| El Paso Electric Company (EE) | 06/12/2015 | 0.295 | 1.18 | 06/16/2015 | 05/29/2015 | 06/30/2015 |
| Endurance Specialty Holdings Ltd (ENH) | 06/12/2015 | 0.35 | 1.4 | 06/16/2015 | 05/21/2015 | 06/30/2015 |
| Equity One, Inc. (EQY) | 06/12/2015 | 0.22 | 0.88 | 06/16/2015 | 05/21/2015 | 06/30/2015 |
| ESSA Bancorp, Inc. (ESSA) | 06/12/2015 | 0.09 | 0.36 | 06/16/2015 | 06/01/2015 | 06/30/2015 |
| First Financial Bankshares, Inc. (FFIN) | 06/12/2015 | 0.16 | 0.64 | 06/16/2015 | 05/04/2015 | 07/01/2015 |
| Fidelity National Information Services, Inc. (FIS) | 06/12/2015 | 0.26 | 1.04 | 06/16/2015 | 04/29/2015 | 06/30/2015 |
| Fidelity National | 06/12/2015 | 0.19 | 0.76 | 06/16/2015 | 05/05/2015 | 06/30/2015 |

Use whichever website you prefer, just be sure you remember the dates and when you have to be the owner of a stock in order to receive a dividend.

# Chapter 3

## Other important terms and facts you should know

Apart from 4 different dividend dates there are a dozen other important terms that you should know, because knowledge of it will impact how you invest and select your dividend paying stocks. Let's look at some of them.

## Dividend

A dividend is sharing of company's earning with its shareholders by means cash, stock or property. It can be paid annually, once in half a year or in most cases quarterly.

## Cash Dividends

Cash dividends are often called simply dividends and they are paid on per share basis. The size of dividend is calculated according to current value of the shares and is decided by the Board of directors.

## Dividend Coverage Ratio

It is ratio between earnings of a company and the net dividend that it pays to its shareholders. This ratio is essential as the sum of dividends that company pays cannot exceed company's earnings. If it does, there could be something suspicious about the company. It may be willing to push up its share price or attract new investors at the expense of higher dividends. Good companies do pay dividends, but they are always within the limits of sound mind and they never exceed a company's earnings. You can calculate this ratio by dividing earnings per share by the dividend per share.

## Dividend Reinvestment Plan (Known as DRIP)

Some dividend paying companies provide their investors with a possibility to automatically reinvest the dividends that they get in order to purchase extra shares of the stock and that usually happens on the day when dividends are paid.

## Dividend Yield

It is another vary important financial indicator that shows a ratio how much of dividends are paid by a company each year in comparison to the stock share price. You can calculate the yield of a given stock by dividing yearly dividend per share by the current price of the stock.

How to calculate a stock dividend yield?

Here is a simple illustrated dividend yield calculation formula:

Dividend Yield = $\underline{\text{Yearly Dividends Per Share}}$

                      Price Per Share

Let's say a stock ABC is at 100$ per share and the yearly dividend for the stock is 3$ per share. The dividend yield for ABC shares would be 3 percent. If the price of shares rises and the dividend remains the same, the yield for the shares automatically decreases. Let's say the price of shares for ABC stock rises to 200$ per share, but the dividend remains 3$ per share. The yield for the stock is then 1.5 percent.

On the other hand, if the price of shares falls, but the dividend remains the same, the dividend yield for the shares increases. Let's say the price of shares for ABC company falls to 30$ per share. According to our calculation, the yield for the shares of the stock is then 10 percent.

Some investors become fascinated by high yielding dividend stocks. However, one should be very careful about companies that offer a very high yield. It might not be such a safe investment after all. It is usually assumed that high yields are often followed by low growth in the future, meaning companies see slowing growth and they want to keep their investors by offering higher yield. An even more worrisome situation is when a company offers extremely high yields that exceed its earnings. This may mean that the company is in trouble and may start cutting dividends sooner rather than later or even stop paying them in the nearest future due to the troubles that it faces. It is commonly accepted that stable and reliable companies have between 2-5 percent dividend yields.

## Effective yield

Effective yield helps an investor to know what the real current yield is based on the amount of money he actually paid for the stock. If the stock that you own trades at 100 and the company pays 4 dollar for a share, current yield is 4 percent. However, if you bought the shares of the company at 50$ current yield (effective yield) for the stock that you own is 8 percent. It is important to understand this; because higher yields may not be that attractive if you bought shares at a high price (near a peak). On the other hand, if you bought them low you should be very happy as you are making money on the growth of the shares as well as from the high dividend yield.

## One Time Dividend

This is the type of dividend that is paid in addition to regular dividends. Companies may decide to share extra earnings with their shareholders for whatever reason they decide. No need to say it is very good for an average shareholder.

## Shareholder

Shareholder is a person, a company or any other institution that owns shares (at least one) of a given stock company.

## Cash dividends or stock dividends

When investors talk about dividends, they usually mean cash dividends. Each shareholder gets money for each share depending on current percent of dividend. It may be represented to investors in terms of amount of dollars per share or in terms of percentage of current market value. Shareholders get cash that is deducted from company's earning and profits. Those who are interested in long term investments will probably reinvest the cash that they get from dividends in order to purchase more shares of the company in order to get more dividends next time. And that they will reinvest again. And so the circle will continue till an investor decides what he wants to do with the money he has made over the years from dividends.

Stock dividends are not cash. If shareholders are paid in stocks rather than cash, they get extra shares of a company. The number of shares that you will get will depend on the number of shares you own at the moment. The company may issue a dividend that equals 3 shares for every 100 shares you are the owner of. So, if you have 1000 shares, you will get 30 more shares, based on the principle described above.

## Annual, quarterly and monthly dividends

There is no one single accepted standard as to how often dividends should be paid. However, over the years some patterns have emerged and most corporations (at least in the USA) pay quarterly dividends.

On the other hand, outside of the USA most companies pay annual dividends, that is: they pay only one time per year.

Monthly dividends are also not an exception. In fact, there are hundreds of companies that pay dividends each month. Whichever way you prefer is up to you. Select the best companies, whether they pay annually, quarterly or monthly and start investing.

Below is the chart from dividend.com that shows how you can find companies that pay monthly dividends. At the time of writing, there are 752 companies that pay monthly dividends. You may go to the site and browse through all of them by choosing criteria: alphabetical order, according to dividend.com DARS''' rating, according to highest dividend yield, company name or ex-dividend date.

**Source: dividend.com**

| Stock Symbol | Company Name | DARS™ Rating [?] | Dividend Yield** | Current Price* | Annualized Dividend | Ex-Div Date | Pay Date |
|---|---|---|---|---|---|---|---|
| ACG | AllianceBernstein Income Fund Inc | Login/Signup for Ratings | 5.47% | 7.49 | 0.41 | 6/3/2015 | 6/19/2015 |
| ACP | Avenue Income Credit Strategies Fund | Login/Signup for Ratings | 9.80% | 14.70 | 1.44 | 6/9/2015 | 6/30/2015 |
| AFB | AllianceBernstein National Municipal Income Fund, Inc. | Login/Signup for Ratings | 5.95% | 13.30 | 0.79 | 6/3/2015 | 6/19/2015 |
| AFT | Apollo Senior Floating Rate Fund Inc | Login/Signup for Ratings | 6.47% | 18.12 | 1.17 | 6/16/2015 | 6/30/2015 |
| AGC | Advent/Claymore Global Convertible Securities & Income Fund | Login/Signup for Ratings | 8.47% | 6.61 | 0.56 | 6/11/2015 | 6/30/2015 |
| AGD | Alpine Global Dynamic Dividend Fund | Login/Signup for Ratings | 7.64% | 10.21 | 0.78 | 6/19/2015 | 6/30/2015 |
| AGG | iShares Barclays Aggregate Bond Fund | Login/Signup for Ratings | 2.05% | 108.89 | 2.23 | 6/1/2015 | 6/5/2015 |
| AGND | WisdomTree Trust | Login/Signup for Ratings | 1.45% | 45.60 | 0.66 | 5/22/2015 | 5/29/2015 |
| AGZ | iShares Barclays Agency Bond | Login/Signup for Ratings | 1.28% | 112.86 | 1.45 | 6/1/2015 | 6/5/2015 |
| AGZD | WisdomTree Trust | Login/Signup for Ratings | 1.60% | 48.80 | 0.78 | 5/22/2015 | 5/29/2015 |
| AIF | Apollo Tactical Income Fund Inc | Login/Signup for Ratings | 8.66% | 16.16 | 1.40 | 6/16/2015 | 6/30/2015 |

## Understanding the power of dividend reinvestment

Investors can really experience the power of compounding by reinvesting their dividends. It has already been stated in the first chapter that one can become rich if he spends some 25 years reinvesting his dividends to buy more stocks. This is even more powerful with companies that have been increasing their dividends year after year. You will find the list of these special companies in the chapters about dividend aristocrats and dividend kings. Of course, you will most probably pay taxes on those (depends on the country you live in), but your money will be employed non-stop, which will grow the value of your portfolio quarter after quarter and year after year.

Website buyupside.com has an excellent tool: dividend reinvestment tool that will help you to calculate how much your investment will grow in value if you reinvest your dividends in comparison to how it will look like if you don't.

We chose our own parameters that you can see in the first table and you can compare for yourself how your investment would differ if you chose to reinvest your dividends and how ti will look like without doing that. Here is the table below!

**Dividend Reinvestment Calculator (from buyupside.com)**

| Dividend Reinvestment Calculator | |
| --- | --- |
| Initial Number of Shares: | 100 |
| Initial Stock Price per Share: | $ 50 |
| Annual Dividend: | $ 3 |
| Dividend Annual Growth Rate: | 5 % |
| Stock Price Annual Growth Rate: | 5 % |
| Number of Years: | 25 |

Calculate    Reset

| Calculator Results | Without Dividend Reinvestment | With Dividend Reinvestment |
| --- | --- | --- |
| Total Value | $31,965.81 | $72,668.99 |
| Number Shares | 100.00 | 429.19 |
| Dividends Paid | $15,034.04 | $37,726.96 |
| Annualized Return | 7.7 % | 11.3 % |

Had you been buying more shares each year or quarter you would probably be a millionaire if not multimillionaire after 25 years. You can go to the website of buyupside.com to do your own calculations. Choose your favorite stocks and play around by entering data and seeing for yourself how your money compounds with the help of dividend reinvestment.

## Dividend capturing strategy

One should be familiar with the fact that buying a stock well in advance of dividends payment is not the only way investors use. It is obvious that investing in dividends is one of the most secure and conservative way to play the stock market. However, even in dividend stocks you can do some short term moves in order to get a dividend and then sell the stock quickly back to the market.

In most cases, after the dividend is received the stock drops by an equivalent amount of dollars and readjusts itself. However, this is not always the case. A stock may drop by a smaller amount, or it may actually start rising after initial drop and end a day somewhat higher. So, a short term speculator may sell back the stock with dividends in his hands and a small loss in share price (which is smaller than the profits from dividends).

Despite the fact, this looks appealing for most traders who want fast profits, these strategies do not win all the time and one has to be very skillful to trade dividend stocks in such a way. It is much more useful and profitable to trade in a conservative way and accumulate profits in the long run.

## Some facts about taxes on dividends

It depends on a country's laws how it taxes or doesn't dividends. These laws change too. At some point dividends can be tax exempt, but if country stores up a lot of public debts it may start searching things it can tax and dividends can become one of them.

Another thing you should know is that countries typically sign double taxation treaties meaning that if you make dividends in one country, you only pay taxes on them in your home country in order to avoid being taxed in the country dividends originate and in the country they are paid to. You need to check your local laws and how it related to investment abroad if you are not a US citizen.

Double taxation idea (taxes paid in two countries) should not be confused with the idea of income being taxed and then dividends being taxed. That is also called double taxation. As most companies that have been paying dividends for long years are in US you should know how dividends were and are taxed in US. Below is the chart showing time periods and tax rates on dividends from the early 20th century up to now.

## History of tax rates on dividends in US

| Time Period | Tax rate on dividends |
| --- | --- |
| 1913-1936 | No tax |
| 1936-1939 | Individual income tax rate (Maximum 79 %) |
| 1939-1953 | No tax |
| 1954-1985 | Individual income tax rate (Maximum 90 %) |
| 1985-2003 | Individual income tax rate (Maximum 28-50 %) |
| 2003-Present | 15% |

# Chapter 4

# Companies that have been paying dividends for over one hundred years

Since investing in dividend stocks is all about security and stability it would be interesting to know whether there have been companies that have been paying dividends for a hundred years or more uninterrupted. You would be surprised, but there were and are such companies. Within a period of 100 years the world saw two world wars, a dozen of global financial as well as economic crises and a lot of worldwide political turmoil. However, there were companies that were paying dividends without interruptions through all of the mess the world was in during those times. I do not know how about you; but that types of companies do catch my attention and if I was considering which dividend paying companies to invest to these would surely be on my list. Let's look at both American and Canadian companies that have shared their profits with their investors by means of dividends for more than one hundred years. The list is presented from top to bottom: from those that started later to those that started earlier. Here are the companies with their stock symbol, year dividends have been paid since, consecutive increases of dividends and current yield!

**1 Chubb Corp.** (CB)
Dividends paid since: 1902. Consecutive increases of dividends: 45. Current yield: 2.92%

**2 PPG** (PPG) Dividends paid since: 1899. Consecutive increases of dividends: 36.  Current yield: 3.55%

**3 Colgate-Palmolive Company** (CL)
Dividends paid since: 1895. Consecutive increases of dividends: 45. Current yield: 2.13%

**4 The Coca-Cola Company** (KO).
Dividends paid since: 1893. Consecutive increases of dividends: 47. Current yield: 3.02%

**5 The Procter & Gamble Company**
Dividends paid since: 1891. Consecutive increases of dividends: 53. Current yield: 2.92%

**6 UGI Corp.** (UGI).
Dividends paid since: 1885. Consecutive increases of dividends: 23. Current yield: 3.20%

**7 Consolidated Edison, Inc.** (ED.
Dividends paid since: 1885. Consecutive increases of dividends: 36. Current yield: 5.42%

**8 Eli Lilly and Company** (LLY)
Dividends paid since: 1885. Consecutive increases of dividends: 42.  Current Yield: 5.52%

**9 Exxon Mobil Corp.** (XOM).
Dividends paid since: 1882. Consecutive increases of dividends: 27. Current yield: 2.51%

**10 Stanley Works** (SWK).
Dividends paid since: 1877.  Consecutive increases of dividends: 42. Current yield: 2.44%


For the sake of diversification you might also look at foreign companies that have been paying dividends for over one hundred years.

## Canadian companies that have paid dividends for over 100 years

Bank of Montreal (BMO) – paid dividends since 1829.

Bank of Nova Scotia (BNS) – paid dividends since 1832.

TD (TD) – paid dividends since 1857.

CIBC (CM) – paid dividends since 1868.

Royal Bank (RY) – paid dividends since 1870.

# Chapter 5

## Dividend aristocrats: invest in companies that have been increasing dividends for over 25 years

A dividend aristocrat is a company that has been paying and increasing dividends for 25 years. Imagine owning one of these stocks for over 25 years and reinvesting the dividends to buy more of the stock. That would be a real realization of compounding. You would definitely be rich by now. Those who have done thorough research tell us that dividend aristocrat companies have beaten S&P 500 index since 1989, which means that would have got bigger profits by buying and holding managers are not able to beat the stock index on a yearly basis. It may mean that would do much better by investing in the index, rather than giving your money to some fund manager. It may also mean that you'd simply better buy dividend aristocrats and hold them for your own financial benefits. Anyway, these special companies are better to invest to than buying and holding S&P 500 index. Just for your knowledge: these companies do exist and it is worth knowing who they are and possibly putting them in your investment portfolio.

Of course, there are a limited number of those, but you can still find them in various market sectors, which means if you want to invest in different sectors while purchasing stocks you can surely diversify and reduce your risk in case one day some of the companies stop increasing their dividends or stop paying them.

Currently, you can find dividend aristocrats in ten different market sectors. Right after crises (in 2010) there was a decrease in the number of these companies as ten companies out of fifty two dropped from the list. In a matter of next three years the list increased again to fifty four companies.

The list may change again in a matter of a few years, but as of now the full number of companies is right below with their symbols:

1. 3M Company (MMM)
2. AFLAC Inc. (AFL)
3. AbbVie Inc. – (ABBV)
4. Abbott Laboratories (ABT)
5. Air Products & Chemicals Inc (APD)
6. Archer-Daniels-Midland Co (ADM)
7. AT&T (T)
8. Automatic Data Processing (ADP)

9. Bard, C.R. Inc (BCR)

10. Becton, Dickinson & Co (BDX)

11. Bemis Co Inc (BMS)

12. Brown-Forman Corp B (BF/B)

13. Cardinal Health Inc. – (CAH)

14. Chubb Corp (CB)

15. Chevron Corp. – (CVX)

16. Cincinnati Financial Corp (CINF)

17. Cintas Corp (CTAS)

18. Clorox Co (CLX)

19. Coca-Cola Co (KO)

20. Colgate-Palmolive (CL)

21. Consolidated Edison Inc (ED)

22. Dover Corp (DOV)

23. Ecolab Inc (ECL)

24. Emerson Electric Co (EMR)

25. Exxon Mobil Corp (XOM)

26. Family Dollar Stores Inc (FDO)

27. Franklin Resources (BEN)

28. Genuine Parts (GPC)

29. Grainger, W.W. Inc (GWW)

30. HCP (HCP)

31. Hormel Foods Corp (HRL)

32. Illinois Tool Works (ITW)

33. Johnson & Johnson (JNJ)

34. Kimberly-Clark (KMB)

35. Leggett & Platt (LEG)

36. Lowe's Cos Inc (LOW)

37. McCormick & Co (MKC)

38. McDonald's Corp (MCD)

39. McGraw-Hill Cos Inc (MHFI)

40. Medtronic (MDT)

41. Nucor (NUE)

42. PPG Industries Inc (PPG)

43. PepsiCo Inc (PEP)

44. Pentair Ltd. – (PNR)

45. Procter & Gamble (PG)

46. Sherwin-Williams Co (SHW)

47. Sigma-Aldrich Corp (SIAL)

48. Stanley Black & Decker Inc. (SWK)

49. Sysco (SYY)

50. T. Rowe Price (TROW)

51. Target Corporation (TGT)

52. VF Corporation (VFC)

53. Walmart (WMT)

54. Walgreen Company (WBA)

## Be selective

As you may see the list contains such known brands as AT&T, Chevron, Coca-Cola, Exxon Mobil or Walmart. If you have enough cash you can actually invest in all of them. However, most of us will probably not have that much money. We will have to be selective. What can we base our selection on?

# Choose highest yielding aristocratic stocks

One of the ways is to look through the list and find the stocks that have the highest yield. We live in financial environment where interest rates are low and keeping money in the bank won't give you return you expect. In fact, in some countries in Europe you will actually have now to pay up to the bank for it to keep your money, because interest rates are at record lows. Highest yielding aristocrat stocks could be a temporary solution for that.

Below is the list of 12 companies that were highest yielding aristocrat stocks in 2014. You may want to look through them and possibly buy one or a few of them. The list was published in marketwatch.com. AT&T tops the list.

| Company | Ticker | Industry | Closing price - Oct. 28 | Annual dividend | Dividend yield |
|---|---|---|---|---|---|
| AT&T Inc. | T, -0.03% | Telecommunications | $34.33 | $1.84 | 5.36% |
| HCP Inc. | HCP, -1.69% | Real Estate Investment Trusts | $43.37 | $2.18 | 5.03% |
| Consolidated Edison Inc. | ED, -0.31% | Electric Utilities | $62.88 | $2.52 | 4.01% |
| McDonald's Corp. | MCD, +0.15% | Restaurants | $92.60 | $3.40 | 3.67% |
| Chevron Corp. | CVX, -0.59% | Integrated Oil | $117.13 | $4.28 | 3.65% |
| Cincinnati Financial Corp. | TGT, +0.37% CINF, -0.76% | Property/ Casualty Insurance | $49.31 | $1.76 | 3.57% |
| Target Corp. | TGT, +0.37% | Discount Stores | $60.65 | $2.08 | 3.43% |
| AbbVie Inc. | ABBV, +0.80% | Major Pharmaceuticals | $60.93 | $1.96 | 3.22% |
| Leggett & Platt Inc. | LEG, +0.53% | Home Furnishings | $38.78 | $1.24 | 3.20% |
| Sysco Corp. | SYY, -0.03% | Food Distributors | $38.20 | $1.16 | 3.04% |
| Clorox Co. | CL, -0.28% CLX, -0.05% | Household/ Personal Care | $97.80 | $2.96 | 3.03% |
| Coca-Cola co. | KO, -0.41% | Beverages: Non-alcoholic | $40.56 | $1.22 | 3.01% |

Source: marketwatch.com

You should also know that you can do your own analysis of each dividend aristocrat companies according to various pieces of criteria. Buypside.com has a special category on these special companies and you can analyze them from various angles: annual dividend yield, industry, 1 year price chart, 10 year moving average (technical indicator), first year of dividend increase, dividend chart, return calculator, return map and a lot more. Here is a chart from the website with all of the companies that belong to dividend aristocrat list.

| Dividend Aristocrats (Sorted by Dividend Yield) | | | | | | | | | |
|---|---|---|---|---|---|---|---|---|---|
| Stock (A-Z) | Price Quote | Annual Dividend & Yield | Industry | 1-Year Price Chart | 10-Year Moving Average | First Year of Dividend Increase | Dividend Chart* | Return Calculator* | Return Map* |
| HCP | HCP | 2.26 (6.00%) | REIT - Healthcare | | | 1986 | | | |
| AT&T | T | 1.88 (5.40%) | Telecom Services | | | 1985 | | | |
| Consolidated Edison | ED | 2.60 (4.50%) | Diversified Utilities | | | 1975 | | | |
| Chevron | CVX | 4.28 (4.30%) | Integrated Oil and Gas | | | 1988 | | | |
| Cincinnati Financial Corporation | CINF | 1.84 (3.60%) | Property & Casualty Insurance | | | 1961 | | | |
| McDonald's | MCD | 3.40 (3.60%) | Restaurants | | | 1977 | | | |
| Procter & Gamble | PG | 2.65 (3.40%) | Personal Products | | | 1957 | | | |
| ExxonMobil | XOM | 2.92 (3.40%) | Integrated Oil and Gas | | | 1983 | | | |
| Coca-Cola | KO | 1.32 (3.30%) | Beverages - Soft | | | 1963 | | | |
| Kimberly-Clark | KMB | 3.52 (3.30%) | Personal Products | | | 1973 | | | |

| Company | Ticker | Dividend (Yield) | Industry | | Since | | |
|---|---|---|---|---|---|---|---|
| **Sysco** | SYY | 1.20 (3.20%) | Wholesale Food | | 1971 | | |
| **Emerson** | EMR | 1.88 (3.20%) | Diversified Electronics | | 1957 | | |
| **AbbVie** | ABBV | 2.04 (3.10%) | Drugs and Biotech | Not Enough P | 2013 | | |
| **Johnson&Johnson** | JNJ | 3.00 (3.10%) | Drugs and Biotech | | 1963 | | |
| **Nucor** | NUE | 1.49 (3.10%) | Steel and Iron | | 1974 | | |
| **PepsiCo** | PEP | 2.81 (3.00%) | Beverages - Soft | | 1973 | | |
| **Clorox** | CLX | 3.08 (2.90%) | Housewares | | 1978 | | |
| **Target** | TGT | 2.24 (2.80%) | Discount Stores | | 1968 | | |
| **Wal-Mart Stores** | WMT | 1.96 (2.70%) | Department Stores | | 1975 | | |
| **Genuine Parts** | GPC | 2.46 (2.70%) | Auto Parts Wholesale | | 1957 | | |
| **T Rowe Price** | TROW | 2.08 (2.60%) | Asset Management | | 1987 | | |
| **3M** | MMM | 4.10 (2.60%) | Conglomerates | | 1959 | | |
| **Leggett & Platt** | LEG | 1.24 (2.60%) | Home Goods | | 1972 | | |
| **Aflac** | AFL | 1.56 (2.50%) | Accident & Health Insurance | | 1983 | | |

| | | | | | | | |
|---|---|---|---|---|---|---|---|
| **Automatic Data Processing** | ADP | 1.96 (2.40%) | Business Software | | 1975 | | |
| **Chubb Corporation** | CB | 2.28 (2.30%) | Property & Casualty Insurance | | 1966 | | |
| **Colgate-Palmolive** | CL | 1.52 (2.30%) | Personal Products | | 1964 | | |
| **Dover Corp** | DOV | 1.60 (2.20%) | Diversified Machinery | | 1956 | | |
| **Air Products** | APD | 3.24 (2.20%) | Chemicals | | 1983 | | |
| **Archer-Daniels-Midland** | ADM | 1.12 (2.20%) | Agribusiness | | 1976 | | |
| **Illinois Tool Works** | ITW | 1.94 (2.10%) | Diversified Machinery | | 1964 | | |
| **Pentair Ltd.** | PNR | 1.28 (2.10%) | Industrial Equipment | | 1977 | | |
| **W.W. Grainger** | GWW | 4.68 (2.00%) | Industrial Equipment | | 1972 | | |
| **McCormick** | MKC | 1.60 (2.00%) | Processed Food | | 1987 | | |
| **Abbott Laboratories** | ABT | 0.96 (2.00%) | Drugs and Biotech | | 1973 | | |
| **Stanley Works** | SWK | 2.08 (2.00%) | Machine Tools | | 1968 | | |
| **VF Corp** | VFC | 1.28 (1.80%) | Apparel | | 1973 | | |

| | | | | | | | |
|---|---|---|---|---|---|---|---|
| **Hormel** | HRL | 1.00 (1.80%) | Meat Products | | 1967 | | |
| **BD (Becton, Dickinson and Company)** | BDX | 2.40 (1.70%) | Medical Instruments & Supplies | | 1972 | | |
| **Cardinal Health** | CAH | 1.55 (1.70%) | Drug Services | | 1989 | | |
| **Lowe's** | LOW | 1.12 (1.60%) | Home Improvement Stores | | 1963 | | |
| **Family Dollar** | FDO | 1.24 (1.60%) | Discount Stores | | 1977 | | |
| **Walgreen Company** | WBA | 1.35 (1.60%) | Drug Stores | | 1976 | | |
| **Brown-Forman** | BF-B | 1.40 (1.60%) | Beverages - Alcoholic | | 1985 | | |
| **Medtronic** | MDT | 1.22 (1.60%) | Medical Equipment | | 1978 | | |
| **McGraw-Hill** | MHFI | 1.32 (1.30%) | Business Services | | 1974 | | |
| **Franklin Resources** | BEN | 0.60 (1.20%) | Asset Management | | 1982 | | |
| **Ecolab** | ECL | 1.32 (1.20%) | Cleaning Products | | 1986 | | |
| **PPG Industries** | PPG | 1.44 (1.20%) | Specialty Chemicals | | 1973 | | |
| **Cintas** | CTAS | 0.85 (1.00%) | Business Services | | 1984 | | |
| **Sherwin-Williams** | SHW | 2.68 (1.00%) | Specialty Chemical | | 1979 | | |

| | | | s | | | | |
|---|---|---|---|---|---|---|---|
| **Sigma-Aldrich** | SIAL | 0.92 (0.70%) | Specialty Chemicals | | 1976 | | |
| **C. R. Bard** | BCR | 0.96 (0.60%) | Medical Instruments and Supplies | | 1972 | | |

Source: **buyupside.com**

# Chapter 6

## Dividend Kings: companies that have increased dividends for fifty or more years

It is good to know about companies that have been paying their investors for 25 years or more. As you know by now, that there are 54 of such companies. This list changes from time to time, but it usually increases, not decreases, so there are much higher chances that these companies will keep on increasing those dividends rather than start cutting them.

Now, dividend aristocrats are really cool, but what if there still is a better class of stocks you could invest in. And you know what, there actually is. There are companies that have been increasing dividends for fifty years or more. Investors tend to call these **dividend kings**. At the moment there are 16 companies that belong to the category. Some of them are very famous brands that will be known not only in the USA and the Western World, but probably in Africa or even Antarctica (among penguins). Just joking! Let's better see what companies are on the list and give a few details about each one of them. Since they are in this category it is good to know at least some fundamentals about them. So, let's look at the companies in the last chapter of the EBook!

**American States Water Company (AWR)**

This is a utility company with probably the lowest market capitalization of roughly a billion and a half. The real success of the company lies in the fact that it has been able to make long term contracts guaranteeing a stream of cash for decades into the future. As you may understand this gives stability for the company and trust for investors. The company has also been increasing its dividends for 60 years and the dividend yield is now 2.3 percent. You can see from the chart below that the stock of AWR rose sharply in 2014 and has been going down slightly in 2015.

**Cincinnati Financial (CINF)**

It is a US casualty insurance company with a pretty small market cap of slightly more than 8 billion US dollars. The company has been paying dividends for 53 years and their current dividend yield is quite high at around 3.5 percent. As all insurance companies have to invest, so does Cincinnati Financial. It holds around thirty percent of their portfolio in blue chip companies.

It is another company that often depends on economy and does much better when global economy is in good shape and not so good when it turns down. A high dividend yield and a few other factors may mean that the company may not be able to keep on going increasing its dividends for a long time and dividend cuts may come any time. Anyway, it has been increasing them for over fifty years now and dividend cut may not be around the corner this or next year. From the chart below you can see that CINF rose for the most considerably in 2014 and has been going sideways in 2015.

## Coca-Cola (KO)

The company has been increasing its dividends for 54 years. As you may have noticed in the chapter about dividend aristocrats Coca-Cola has quite high dividend yield, which should definitely attract more investors seeking higher income in this low interest environment when keeping money in the bank is actually losing money slowly but surely. It has hundreds of various brands that are sold all over the world and make hundreds of millions of dollars for the company each year. Looking at current stand of the company in the industry of carbonated and non carbonated drinks as well as non alcoholic beverages we may say that there isn't a shadow of doubt that the company will continue increasing and paying nice dividends to its shareholders. From the chart below you can see that KO rose in 2014 and has been in a moderate range in 2015.

## Colgate-Palmolive (CL)

The company has been increasing dividends for 51 years. It is also another company that has paid dividends for over one hundred years. It may not be among the largest corporations in the world, but it is surely well known everywhere. I mean, who doesn't know Colgate toothpaste? In this market segment it has the biggest share. The company has invested a vast amount of money in advertising, which means they expect to expand and grab a greater market share in the area they specialize. Besides, it is a really global company and with new markets opening every day we can justly expect that they will keep on increasing their dividends. If you look at the chart of CL you can see that it has been in a bullish trend for a few years and the trend will possibly continue.

## Dover Corporation (DOV)

The company is much smaller than most of the dividend kings' companies. Its market capitalization is a little bit smaller than twelve billion US dollars. However, the company has been increasing its dividends for 59 consecutive years.

It has been operating in four different areas: energy, engineered systems, fluids and refrigeration as well as food equipment. As the company has been operating for a very long time it has managed to develop intellectual property and gain trust among other companies and consumers.

After rising in 2013 and most part of 2014 DOV has been consolidating in 2015.

## Emerson Electric (EMR)

It is a manufacturing company with a capitalization just over forty billion US dollars. The company has been increasing its dividends for 57 years. Although market cap is not that big Emerson Electric really contributes to creating jobs across the world as it currently employs around one hundred and thirty thousand people. Like most manufacturing companies it largely depends on a general state of global economy and may suffer slower growth if economy is in recession. However, even during the last crisis it has managed to maintain increase of dividends, which suggests that they will keep on doing as economic situation clears up. Dividend yield of Emerson Electric is now 3.1 percent.

By looking at EMR chart you can see that the stock is not in particularly good shape. It has been going sideways since 2014. In fact, it has been in a downward sloping channel for over a year. It does need to find support (bottom) before one can buy the stock at a better price.

## Genuine Parts Company (GPC)

The company owns its own NAPA stores that sell auto parts and this makes up more than fifty percent of its revenues. It may seem pretty unusual for such kind of business to be very profitable for long, but it is true for Genuine Parts Company that has been increasing its dividends 58 years. It has been a local North American company for long, but for a couple of years now it has been expanding abroad, particularly to Australia and New Zealand markets. If the company continues going in the same direction we can certainly expect a non-stop increase in dividends.

Like most of the dividend kings GPC rose in 2014, but went down slightly in 2015 and has been consolidating for a few months now. By looking at technical picture we may assume that it is at a good level to buy and hold.

## Johnson & Johnson (JNJ)

The company has been increasing its dividends for 52 years. It has tremendous market capitalization that currently stands at around 300 billion dollars. No wonder, it is the biggest healthcare company in the world and one of the largest corporation in the USA. It has three areas of involvement: consumer, pharmaceutical and medical devices as well as diagnostics. It earns over 70 billion dollars in revenue each year from these three areas. As healthcare business is ever expanding, so will the company's income and consequently this will be reflected in more increases of annual dividends.

JNJ rose sharply in years of 2013 and 2014 and has been consolidating for the most part of 2015. It is right at support of 98 level at the moment.

## Lancaster Colony (LANC)

Lancaster Colony is not such an old company as Coca Cola as it was founded in 1961, but it has been paying and increasing dividends for 52 years. It means the company has been successful right from the start. The dividend yield is not very high, but still good: 2 percent. The company sells consumer goods, but has a lot of strong competitors, which means that it is difficult for the company to gain power and grow. Some predict dividend cuts in the nearest future and the company may fall out of dividend kings' list. However, it is still in it and makes nice cash for its shareholders.

It might be the case that LANC stock is in topping formation and will drop at some point in the nearest future. It reached a peak of 97.50 in the beginning of 2014 and was not able to break it since then. The level was revisited in the early part of 2015, but again, price failed to go beyond that level. Wait for lower prices if you intend to buy the stock.

**LANC** Lancaster Colony Corp. Nasdaq GS + BATS
6-Jul-2015 12:17pm     **Open** 90.34 **High** 90.92 **Low** 90.27 **Last** 90.43 **Volume** 11.5K **Chg** -0.39 (-0.43%) ▼
RSI(14) 49.37

LANC (Weekly) 90.43
— MA(50) 89.79
— MA(200) 76.13
Volume 11,470

— MACD(12,26,9) -0.030, 0.087, -0.117

## Lowe's (LOW)

The company specializes in the home improvement area with its major rival being Home Depot. It has been increasing its dividends for 52 years. With close to 2000 stores in the US and market capitalization around 70 billion dollars it really remains the leader in this business. Of course, company's growth is sensitive to business cycles in global economy and particularly in booms and declines in construction area. Therefore, if you buy the shares you may really want to do that when the stock bottoms after a fall. All upcoming booms will surely grow your profits in leaps and bounds and compensate for stagnating stock price when construction sector is in decline.

LOW experienced a very sharp rise in 2014 as it almost doubled in price from May of 2014 till March of 2015. The stock has been consolidating since then. One may wait for a deeper pullback to start buying the stock.

**Nordson Corporation (NDSN)**

Nordson Corporation is a manufacturing company and its business is industrial application equipment. It also belongs to a group of smaller companies among dividend kings with a market capitalization of around 5 billion US dollars. It has been paying dividends for 51 years. However, its current yield is pretty small: 1.16 percent. Despite the fact the company is comparatively small it was able to compete with market giants for over fifty years. For a number of years Nordson Corporation has been repurchasing its shares and also buying other small businesses in the same niche. The company is not in the area that is sensitive to economic downturns and during the last economic meltdown it managed to do relatively well. Taking it into account, we do expect that the company will keep on increasing its dividends for a long time into the future.

If you look at the chart of NDSN you will see that it is not a fast runner. It likes ranges and as its daily volume is not very high it is better to wait till support before buying the stock.

## Northwest Natural Gas (NWN)

Northwest Natural Gas is a utility company that provides gas in the North West. It has been increasing its dividend for 59 years and the current dividend yield is quite high at 3.8 percent. Unfortunately, the niche that the company works in is strictly regulated and profit margins of the company are relatively low. Earnings per share have been increasing steadily, but the dividends have grown even more. It means that sooner or later this kind of rally should stop as no company can increase dividends at the expense of earnings per share. It is surely a company to invest in for those that are chasing higher yields. Again, as the stock belongs to this special group it is much safer to invest in it as most companies that offer very high yields might be doing it only to attract investors. Unfortunately, the stock has been falling for the most part of 2015 after a nice ride upwards in 2014. So, a smart investor would consider waiting for bottoming formation before actually buying this stock.

NWN is a stock that sees larger swings and is not heavily traded. It has been falling for the most part of 2015 and might be at a good level to buy as it currently is at support of 42 level which held for the most part of 2014 when stock broke upwards.

## Parker Hannifin (PH)

The company is in manufacturing business. It has been increasing its dividends for 58 years and current dividend yield is 2 percent. Market capitalization of the company is relatively small in comparison to other dividend kings and is slightly lower than twenty billion US dollars. Like most market leaders the company is leading the way with innovations that increases efficiency of some transport vehicles and commercial aircraft. When the new products will start paying off it will boost company's revenues even more and guarantee further dividend increases.

By looking at the chart below you can see that the stock of PH is well supported at 115 level and that may hold for the rest of the year. It may be the right time and price to buy PH.

## Procter & Gamble (PG)

The company is a champion of a large variety of brands of consumer goods and has been increasing its dividends for 58 years. Taking into account that it belongs to a small group of corporations that have been paying dividends for over one hundred years we may assume that there won't be a slowdown in increase or paying of dividends. Its market capitalization is slightly below 250 billion dollars, which puts it among biggest corporations in the USA and around the world.

At the moment the company is going through restructuring process and tries to get rid of the brands that are less profitable and concentrate on those that are the most profitable. Its stock PG has been falling for the most part of 2015, but it may be close to final bottom for the year as it really displays some bullish signs.

**Vectren Corporation (VVC)**

Vectren Corporation is yet another utilities company with the smallest market capitalization among dividend kings: 3.8 billion US dollars. Current dividend yield is quite good – 3.3 percent. Its utility business is in a limited area, basically Indiana and Ohio. Apart from utilities the company also runs some infrastructure and energy services. Over the past few years' company's growth slowed down a bit, particularly due to strictly regulated utility industry.  It is quite possible that the company will continue growing, but not because of its utilities, but other kind of businesses. It is difficult to expect a nonstop dividend increases in the years to come where low profits margins are placed on business.

That is another stock that rose sharply in 2013 and 2014, yet has been beaten in 2015. The price of VVC is now at support of 38 level, which may hold and if it does, it could be the best place to buy the share of Vectren Corporation.

## 3M (MMM)

3M is a machinery company with a capitalization around one hundred billion dollars. It has been increasing its dividends for 56 years. It specializes in five main areas: industry, electronics and energy, safety and graphics, health care and consumer. Industrial area is the most profitable one as it generates around thirty percent of company's revenues. The company constantly invests in new technology and therefore always has an edge in the market as a result getting big contracts and winning public tenders around the world.

3 MMM ran spectacularly in 2013 and 2014 from 85 $ per share to 170 $ per share meaning you would have made money not only by means of dividends, but also due to rise of the stock. The stock has fallen slightly in 2015 and has been consolidating for a few months now. It might make another rally from here.

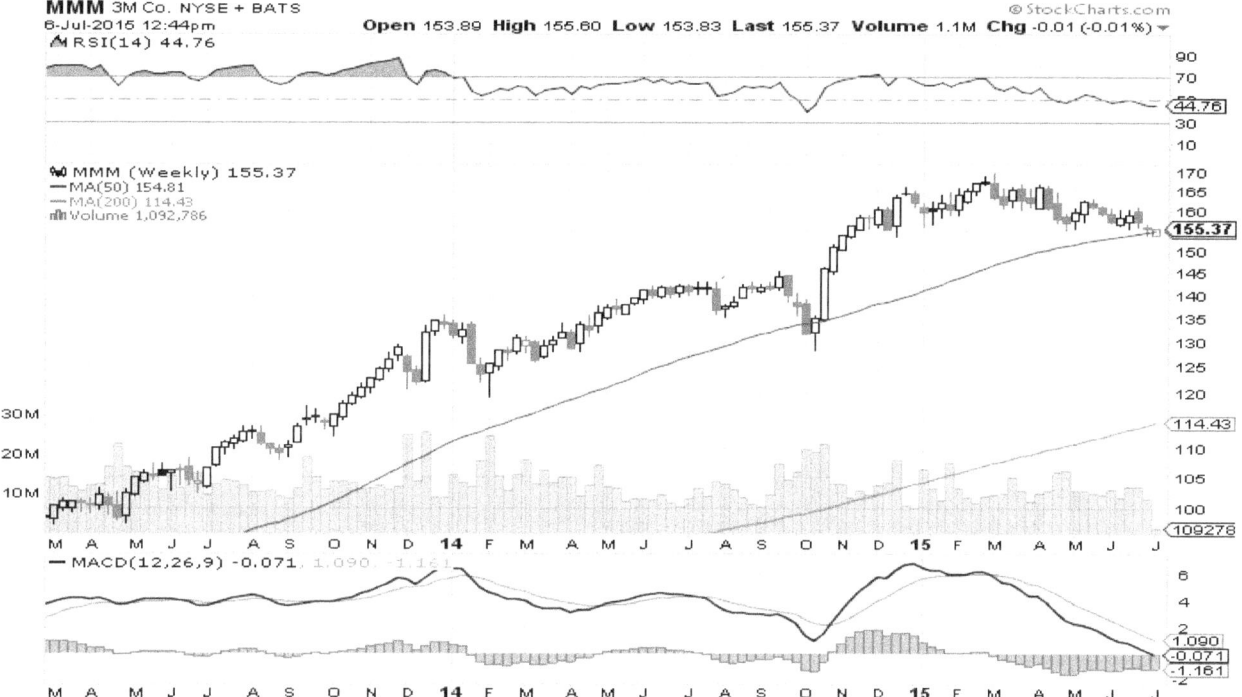

## Conclusion

As you may see, despite the list of dividend kings is not big you can still choose from a number of market sectors, sizes of companies as well as different dividend yields. What you need to know is not to buy these stops at market tops. Wait for a pullback or a counter trend move and then purchase some shares. You may do it in blocks if you see that the stock stopped from dropping and is rising. Anyway, never forget the main rule of investing: buy low and sell high. In our case with dividend stocks you may want to buy low and keep it for years. Good luck in doing that.

Thanks you for your purchsase

Please check out my other book

Forex tradeing for begginers

By

Andrew Fincher